Mastering the Mindset of Self-Love: 28-Day Guided Journal

By Lani Edmonds and Kari Sayers

Copyright © 2017 The Gorgeous Mindset Effect, LLC.

All Rights Reserved.

Published by Think Positive Journals

No part of this publication may be reproduced or stored in a retrieval system or transmitted in any form or by any means, electronic, mechanical, recording, photocopying, scanning, or otherwise without express written consent of the publisher.

The Purpose of This Journal

The purpose of this journal is to support you on your journey to embracing a lifestyle that includes spending more time, energy, and money on yourself.

Inside, you will find 28 activities designed to help you to move closer to living a life that is rich in self-acceptance, self-rejuvenation, and self-love. By the time you complete the journal, you will have:

- A clearer understanding of what self-love looks like in your life
- A better view of what steps you need to take to continue your self-love journey
- An expanded awareness of the unhealthy habits that are blocking your happiness and prosperity
- A deeper perspective on how to create a better relationship with the one person who has supreme power over your life--YOU!

Our goal is that you will use this journal to reflect on your experiences, thoughts, and feelings as it pertains to mastering the mindset of self-love. We believe that journaling your experiences can help with your spiritual, mental, and emotional clarity and we want this journal to be a helpful tool to aid your progress.

For even more inspiration, be sure to sign-up for the Mastering the Mindset of Self-Love free video course. The free course gives extra tips, self-love ideas, and personal stories to help maximize your journaling experience. Sign-up at www.thegorgeousmindseteffect.com.

How It Works

Complete One Activity Each Day

Starting with Day 1 in the Mastering the Mindset of Self-Love Journal, complete one activity each day for 28 days. Set aside a few minutes every morning when you wake up or during your lunch break or before you go to bed at night. If you miss a day, no problem, just pick up where you left off when you're ready to start again.

Watch the Corresponding Video Tip for Each Activity

Each activity has a companion video lesson which you can access for FREE at www.selflovemindset.com. In these videos, we share tips and advice relating to each activity, including some of our personal stories and experiences. These videos are designed to give you a deeper look into the activities and offer additional inspiration and insights.

Write Your Thoughts ad Understandings

Following each activity in the Mastering the Mindset of Self-Love Journal, you will find a blank page where you can write down your thoughts, ideas, feelings, and desires that you have while completing the activity. We suggest spending a few minutes each day reflecting on what that day's activity meant to you.

Contents

Health

Day 1 - Do the Mirror Work	6
Day 2 - Appreciate and Pamper Yourself	9
Day 3 - Complete an Outdoor Activity	12
Day 4 - Disconnect from the World	15
Day 5 - The "I'm Hot, and I Rock" List	18
Day 6 - You Are What You Eat. What Are You?	21
Day 7 - Create a Self-Love Box	24

Relationships

Day 8 - Give Yourself Credit	27
Day 9 - Forgive Yourself	30
Day 10 - Say Goodbye to Grudges	33
Day 11 - Ask Yourself "Does This Bring Me Joy?"	36
Day 12 - Take the Path to Self-Approval	39
Day 13 - Be Around Positive People	42
Day 14 - Explore What Makes You a Badass	45

Money

Day 15 - Examine Your Money Story	48
Day 16 - Tackle Your Money Blocks	51
Day 17 - Give Yourself Permission to Make More Money	54
Day 18 - Pay Yourself First	57
Day 19 - Create a Money Plan for More Happiness	60
Day 20 - Make a Mini-Vision Board for Your Dream Home	63
Day 21 - Write Yourself a Check	64

Spirituality

Day 22 - Reflect on Your Spirituality	67
Day 23 - Create Calm in Your Day	70
Day 24 - Understand Your Guiding Principles	73
Day 25 - Ask the Universe for What You Want	76
Day 26 - Live Intentionally	79
Day 27 - Discover Rituals that Serve You	82
Day 28 - Transform Your Life Through Beliefs	85
50 Self-Love Mantras	90
18 Money Mantras	92
Additional Resources	93

Do the Mirror Work

Wouldn't it be great to look yourself in the mirror and know that you are staring at the woman you always wanted to be? You can.

First, you must start by looking in the mirror and setting daily intentions to make changes where change is needed.

Start small and work your way up. Starting can be as simple as looking in the mirror and saying, "I Love Myself." Speaking these simple words can spark drastic change and get going on your way to discovering who you want to be and the person you want to see staring back at you in the mirror.

Here are some starting points:

- Take 5-10 minutes first thing in the morning or at bedtime for a little introspection
- Do daily mirror work…even if it's just smiling at yourself
- Love and appreciate every inch of your body (even the parts of you that you don't particularly like)
- Use the Mirror of Truth (this means looking inwardly to find the person you want to be outward)

Mastering the Mindset of Self-Love

Day 1 Activity

List 5 aspects of yourself that you're ready to embrace. State why you love them. (Even if you don't love them, write as if you do.)

1.
_____
_____
_____

2.
_____
_____
_____

3.
_____
_____
_____

4.
_____
_____
_____

5.
_____
_____
_____

Day 1 Thoughts and Understandings

_____
_____
_____
_____
_____
_____
_____
_____
_____

<u>Self-Love Note</u>

"I am not beautiful like you, I am beautiful like me."

Appreciate and Pamper Yourself

Most of us rarely take the time to show ourselves appreciation. Rewarding yourself is gratifying and much needed on the path to mastering self-love.

Did you make it to work on time today when you're usually late? Reward yourself. Have you decided to use positive words towards yourself and others? Sounds like a reason to reward yourself.

Start being kinder to yourself by regularly practicing self-gratitude and rewarding yourself for a job well done. Anything can be rewarded; it's all up to you.

Here are a few ideas to reward/pamper yourself:

- A massage
- A manicure/pedicure
- A hair appointment
- A movie
- New perfume

Day 2 Activity

Time to reward yourself for embarking on this self-love journey.

Pick 1 or more rewards, pick up the phone, and set an appointment.

☐ Massage

Date:_____

Time:_____

Place:_____

☐ Manicure/Pedicure

Date:_____

Time:_____

Place:_____

☐ Hair

Date:_____

Time:_____

Place:_____

☐ Makeup

Date:_____

Time:_____

Place:_____

Pamper Me Affirmation

_____

_____

_____

_____

_____

Do I Deserve This?

☐ Yes! I F'ing Deserve This!

☐ Of Course I Deserve This!

☐ Yeah, I'm Doing It Anyway!

Day 2 Thoughts and Understandings

_____

_____

_____

_____

_____

_____

_____

_____

_____

_____

<u>Self-Love Note</u>

"I deserve the world, so I'm gonna give it to myself."

Mastering the Mindset of Self-Love

Complete an Outdoor Activity

Get outside and get moving. Being surrounded by nature can reduce stress, anger, and fear. Nature has the power to increase pleasant feelings. It can also cause a much-needed distraction from our everyday pains and discomforts.

Allow the beauty of nature to heal, soothe, restore, and reconnect you to the best part of you.

Here are some ideas for getting out in nature:

- A walk in the park
- Play shapes with the clouds
- View the night sky
- Go for a bike ride

Mastering the Mindset of Self-Love

Day 3 Activity

List 5 things you will do outdoors this week.

1.

2.

3.

4.

5.

Day 3 Thoughts and Understandings

_____

_____

_____

_____

_____

_____

_____

_____

_____

_____

Self-Love Note

"…and into the forest I go to lose my mind and find my soul."

Disconnect from the World

Turn everything off. Yes, everything—your phone, computer, tablet, television, etc. The constant flow of information from our electronic devices can make it hard to concentrate or relax. Disconnect to reconnect with who you truly are.

Try going to bed early to get a great night's rest. Try creating affirmations that fit the life you want to live (note: read the affirmations in the back of this journal for help).

Disconnecting will allow you to begin the process of reprogramming your conscious and subconscious minds. If you do it enough, life-changing miracles are on your horizon.

Day 4 Activity

List a few ways that you can disconnect and relax.

1.
2.
3.
4.
5.

List a few relaxation affirmations to help in the disconnection process.

1.
2.
3.
4.
5.

Day 4 Thoughts and Understandings

_____

_____

_____

_____

_____

_____

_____

_____

_____

_____

Self-Love Note

"Life is what happens between Wi-Fi signals."

The "I'm Hot, and I Rock" List

With self-love, you are always and forever celebrating you. You learn to acknowledge your accomplishments, strengths, differences, charm, wit, and beauty. You can even start acknowledging your future.

Think about accomplishments you've made or want to make shortly. Create an "I'm Hot, and I Rock" list to celebrate these accomplishments. For future accomplishments, write the list as if they have already happened.

Here are some examples:

- I'm hot, and I rock for loving myself every day.
- I'm hot, and I rock for clean eating and exercising consistently.
- I'm hot, and I rock for keeping positive and motivating people in my inner circle.
- I'm hot, and I rock for treating others how I want them to treat me.

Mastering the Mindset of Self-Love

Day 5 Activity

Create a list of 5 "I'm Hot, and I Rock" statements.

I'm hot, and I rock_____.

I'm hot, and I rock_____.

I'm hot, and I rock_____.

I'm hot, and I rock_____.

I'm hot, and I rock_____.

Mastering the Mindset of Self-Love

Day 5 Thoughts and Understandings

_____

_____

_____

_____

_____

_____

_____

_____

_____

Self-Love Note

"Self-confidence is the best outfit, rock it and own it."

You Are What You Eat. What Are You?

You've heard the term *You Are What You Eat*. If you take this into perspective and look back on your diet over the past couple of days, it might be a little scary.

A key component in getting to wellbeing is making a life change by forever incorporating healthy eating habits into your diet. What you put into your body has influence over how you respond to life and life's challenges. So, it's a great idea to be mindful of what you're eating.

Try creating a visual for yourself that can help give you reminders of how important it is to feed your body what it needs to stay clear minded and energized.

Here are some ideas to get your mind working toward better nutrition:

- Begin a daily food journal of what you currently eat.
- Make changes to your diet where it deems important.
- Incorporate drinking 1 gallon of water a day.
- If feasible, hire a personal nutritionist.
- Do your research on nutritional benefits for your body.

Day 6 Activity

Create a simple food journal to track your daily diet, exercise, and mood. A printable version of this form is available at www.selflovemindset.com.

Breakfast

_____

_____

Snack

_____

_____

Lunch

_____

_____

Snack

_____

_____

Dinner

_____

_____

____/____/____

Daily Workout Plan

Mon   Tue   Wed   Thurs   Fri   Sat   Sun

}————————————{

}————————————{

}————————————{

}————————————{

Measuring Daily Mood

☐ Great Momentum

☐ Pushing Through

☐ Not Feeling It Today

☐ "F" All Of This

Day 6 Thoughts and Understandings

___

Self-Love Note

"A healthy outside starts from the inside." -Robert Urich

Create a Self-Love Box

Create your self-love box and fill it with things that inspire and remind you to love yourself. Fill this box with self-love enhancers that will give you the boost you need in those moments where you feel a little down and out. Opening the box will act as a reminder to yourself about the beautiful journey you are on and help you get back on the right track.

Here are some ideas for your self-love box:

- Your favorite affirmations
- A list of your accomplishments
- Trinkets that remind you to love yourself
- Phone number(s) to a person(s) that will remind you of your journey
- A piece of artwork
- A special perfume
- A book

Day 7 Activity

Create a self-love box.

Ideas to get started:

- ✓ Buy a box (or reuse a box you have) and decorate it
- ✓ Buy a decorative box (craft stores are a great place to look)
- ✓ Create a list of favorite affirmations
- ✓ Create a list of accomplishments
- ✓ Find self-love trinkets like jewelry, scarf, a love rock, book, candy
- ✓ Create list of phone numbers of people you love to talk with
- ✓ Put all your self-love reminders/enhancers in your box

Day 7 Thoughts and Understandings

_____

_____

_____

_____

_____

_____

_____

_____

_____

Self-Love Note

"It's not selfish to love yourself, take care of yourself, and make your happiness a priority. It's necessary." - Mandy Hale

Give Yourself Some Credit

Giving yourself credit and showing yourself love daily is often easier said than done. You've probably realized by now that you are usually your own worst critic. You bash yourself for your mistakes and shortcomings and are harder on yourself than anyone else ever could be.

The good news is that even if it's true that you are your own worst critic, it's also true that you can become your own biggest fan.

No one can love you better than you can love yourself.

Mastering the Mindset of Self-Love

Day 8 Activity

List 10 positive "I Am" words or phrases to describe yourself.

Example: I AM a beautiful person.

I AM_____.

I AM_____.

I AM_____.

I AM_____.

I AM_____.

I AM_____.

I AM_____.

I AM_____.

I AM_____.

I AM_____.

Day 8 Thoughts and Understandings

_____
_____
_____
_____
_____
_____
_____
_____
_____
_____

Self-Love Note

"Don't forget to fall in love with yourself first."

Forgive Yourself

When all is said and done, the most important relationship you have is with yourself. Holding on to negativity from your past—like mistakes and regrets—is harmful to your well-being. In fact, doing this is the opposite of self-love because it can cause self-loathing and possibly even self-harm.

When you begin to forgive yourself, you begin a journey to self-acceptance. It's time to make peace with yourself. Forgive yourself for whatever it is that you are holding on to from your past and move one. You deserve it.

Day 9 Activity

List 3-5 negative memories that you are holding on to. After each one, speak the forgiveness affirmation, "I forgive myself. I move forward in peace and love."

1. _____

I forgive myself. I move forward in peace and love.

2. _____

I forgive myself. I move forward in peace and love.

3. _____

I forgive myself. I move forward in peace and love.

4. _____

I forgive myself. I move forward in peace and love.

5. _____

I forgive myself. I move forward in peace and love.

Mastering the Mindset of Self-Love

Day 9 Thoughts and Understandings

Self-Love Note

"Forgive yourself for not knowing, what you don't know, before you learned it."

Say Goodbye to Grudges

There are a million reasons for why people hold grudges against each other. Sometimes it's a grudge against a parent about something that happened to you as a child. Or maybe a grudge against a sibling or a close friend for not being there when you needed them most. The list goes on and on.

Holding on to grudges and living in the past blocks you from creating new experiences, keeps you from feeling better, and does not fix the issue that created the grudge. It simply blocks you from happiness.

To be truly happy, you must learn to let go of them.

Day 10 Activity

Name one person you are currently holding a grudge against.
_____

What's the reason for the grudge?
_____
_____
_____

What small steps you can take to start to move past this grudge.

1.
_____
_____
_____

2.
_____
_____
_____

3.
_____
_____
_____

Day 10 Thoughts and Understandings

_____

_____

_____

_____

_____

_____

_____

_____

_____

<u>Self-Love Note</u>

"Grudges are a waste of perfect happiness. Laugh when you can, apologize when you should, and let go of what you cannot change."

Ask Yourself, "Does This Bring Me Joy?"

Are you a *Yes Woman*? Do you say yes to everything and everyone? Yes to your family. Yes to your children. Yes to your boss. It's *yes, yes, yes.* You say yes even when you're beyond exhausted and want to say *no, no, no.*

You do things out of a sense of obligation, and over time this can lead to feelings of exhaustion and burnout.

You have to be willing and ready to say no sometimes. The next time you're feeling overwhelmed and compelled to say yes (when you want to say no) ask yourself, "Does this bring me joy?" If the answer is no, then strongly consider not doing it.

Mastering the Mindset of Self-Love

Day 11 Activity

List 3- 5 things you often find yourself doing (out of a sense of obligation) that do not bring you joy or happiness.

1.
_____
_____
_____

2.
_____
_____
_____

3.
_____
_____
_____

4.
_____
_____
_____

5.
_____
_____
_____

Write a BOLD statement that kindly says you will no longer be doing the things that fail to bring you joy.

_____
_____
_____

Day 11 Thoughts and Understandings

_____
_____
_____
_____
_____
_____
_____
_____
_____

Self-Love Note

"Sometimes you have to show people that the things you do for them are optional"

Take the Path to Self-Approval

It's human nature to seek approval from parents, partners, bosses, and friends. However, when you begin to measure your success by what other people think of you, this becomes an unhealthy habit that goes against self-love.

Constantly seeking the approval of others gives someone else the power to put a value on your worth. It can cause you to miss out on opportunities because you put your decision-making power in someone else's hands.

The truth is that you are your source of love. You are your grand approval system. You don't need the peanut gallery's approval to be a success.

Day 12 Activity

Who is the person you most often seek approval from?
_____

Why do you think you need their approval?
_____
_____
_____
_____

Are you willing to let go of the need of this approval?

YES   or   NO

Use this space to acknowledge yourself for a good decision you recently made. Self-acknowledgement is one of the first steps on the path to self-approval.

_____
_____
_____
_____

Day 12 Thoughts and Understandings

_____

_____

_____

_____

_____

_____

_____

_____

_____

_____

Self-Love Note

"The only permission, the only validation, and the only opinion that matters in our quest for greatness is our own."

Day 13

Be Around Positive People

Motivational speaker Jim Rohn famously said, "We are the average of the five people that we spend the most time with." If you are a believer in the Law of Averages, then you know that this law states that the result of any situation is the average of all outcomes.

The truth is that the people around you affect your success and your thoughts (whether you want them to or not). If you are surrounded by a team of negative people, you are more likely to join in on the negativity bandwagon after a while.

Likewise, when you surround yourself with a tribe of positive thinking people who want to see you succeed and thrive, you are more likely to do so.

The company you choose to keep around you have the power to help elevate you or the power to help bring you down.

Day 13 Activity

List the five people you currently hang around or talk to most often. Next, draw a circle to indicate if you consider them to be a *mostly positive person or more negative*. Be honest with yourself and your answers.

1.   (mostly positive / more negative)

2.   (mostly positive / more negative)

3.   (mostly positive / more negative)

4.   (mostly positive / more negative)

5.   (mostly positive / more negative)

Write down 3-5 positive attributes of the tribe of people you desire to have near you.

1.

2.

3.

4.

5.

Day 13 Thoughts and Understandings

_____

_____

_____

_____

_____

_____

_____

_____

_____

Self-Love Notes

"Surround yourself with people that have dreams, desires, and ambition; they'll help you push for and realize your own."

Explore What Makes You a Badass

That's right. We all have a little "badassness" inside of us just waiting for discovery. You might look at yourself and think, "Badass? Who me?"

YES, YOU!

It's not just our favorite celebrities, authors, or actresses who get to wear the title of badass. We all have it, and it's this badassness that is just what we need to tap into to start living our best lives.

It's in there. You just have to be willing to explore it.

Here are a few ideas on how to unleash your inner badass:

1. Invest in yourself
2. Get started before you are ready
3. Stop allowing others to put a value on your worth
4. Do what you love
5. Be a voice for the voiceless
6. Have the audacity to do what others will not
7. Live your life unapologetically

Mastering the Mindset of Self-Love

Day 14 Activity

Write down three reasons you ARE A BADASS. Yes...you have at least three.

1.

2.

3.

Optional: Make a 3-minute or less video of yourself sharing why you are a badass. Keep the video and watch it from time to time when you need a confidence boost.

Feel free to share it in the Think and Grow Gorgeous FB Group. We love to see women embracing their inner badass. Let us celebrate with you!

Day 14 Thoughts and Understandings

_____
_____
_____
_____
_____
_____
_____
_____
_____
_____

Self-Love Note

"There's nothing more badass than being yourself."

Examine Your Money Story

We all have a money story. The environment you grew up in, and the people you grew up around played a major role in shaping your money story—for better or for worse.

For the vast majority of people, your experience with money was likely tinged by negativity. You may have been told things like:

Money is the root of all evil.

Money doesn't grow on trees.

Money can't buy you happiness.

Statements like these made an impression on you way back then and continue to influence how you think about money now.

It's important to understand your money story. Knowing your money story is the first step in creating a healthy financial situation for yourself moving forward.

Day 15 Activity

Read the statements below and write the very first thought that comes to your mind to complete the sentences.

I grew up believing that making money is...

_____
_____
_____

People are rich because...

_____
_____
_____

Money can't...

_____
_____
_____

People are poor because...

_____
_____
_____

If I had more money I would...

_____
_____
_____

Day 15 Thoughts and Understandings

Self-Love Note

"It's safe for me to ignore other people's money blocks."

Tackle Your Money Blocks

Money blocks are beliefs and systems that keep you from attaining the financial success you desire. They are often tied to your money story, making it very important first to understand your money story (see day 15).

Money blocks cause you to struggle with making money. They keep money from flowing to you easily, frequently, and abundantly. Learning to identify and eliminate these money blocks is an act of self-love because it allows you to create a healthier financial situation in your life.

Here are a few common money blocks:

- I'm bad with money
- Saving money is a struggle
- I never have enough money for what I want
- I'm too old to get rich
- I'm too young to get rich

Mastering the Mindset of Self-Love

Day 16 Activities

List 5 money blocks you often find yourself thinking.

1. _____

2. _____

3. _____

4. _____

5. _____

Now, flip them around to be money affirmations. Example "I never have enough money to get what I want." Instead, change this money block to "I always have plenty of money to provide all of my wants and needs."

1. _____

2. _____

3. _____

4. _____

5. _____

Day 16 Thoughts and Understandings

_____
_____
_____
_____
_____
_____
_____
_____
_____
_____

Self-Love Note

"It is safe for me to release my money blocks."

Give Yourself Permission to Make More Money

After you acknowledge your money story and your money blocks, it's time for you to begin crafting a new relationship with money. It's time for you to give yourself permission to prosper, to flourish, and to have an abundance of money flowing into your life.

Creating money mantras is a great way to keep yourself motivated and feeling inspired about your money situation.

Here is a money mantra favorite:

Money Comes Easily and Frequently.

Day 17 Activity

Now it's your turn. Write down a few money mantras to incorporate in your everyday life. If you need a little help, there are some money mantras listed toward the back of this journal. Pick your favorite ones to write here.

1.

2.

3.

4.

5.

6.

7.

8.

Day 17 Thoughts and Understandings

_____
_____
_____
_____
_____
_____
_____
_____
_____

Self-Love Note

"It is safe for me to expect an abundance of money."

Pay Yourself First

As you begin to mend your relationship with money, you also boost your self-confidence and your self-worth. Now it's time to get to work on your net worth.

Saving money and investing money in yourself is one of the most underestimated forms of self-love. Saving money means that you value yourself and your future. It's about exercising your power over money; it doesn't control you, rather you control it.

The "Pay Yourself First" model is nothing new, but nevertheless, it is a simple way to set aside money for savings or investing.

There are several ways to implement it. Here's a simplified way to do it:

Pay yourself the first hour of each work day.

Day 18 Activity

Take the time to figure out what your daily, weekly, and monthly pay amouns are. If you are in a salaried position, break your pay down to hourly.

For example:

$40,000 salary ÷ 52 work weeks in a year ÷ 40 hours a week = $19.23 hourly pay. If you pay yourself for the first hour of 5 work days that equals $96.15 per week.

Now, calculate your hourly pay then multiply it by the number of days you work per week to come up with your "Pay Yourself First (PYF)" number.

$_____hourly pay X _____work days = $_____PYF each week.

List 3-5 ways you can invest in yourself and your future with the money you save.

1. _____
2. _____
3. _____
4. _____
5. _____

Day 18 Thoughts and Understandings

Self-Love Notes

"It's safe to invest in myself."

Create a Money Plan

For many people, just saying the word "budget" is enough to make you cringe. Instead of "budgeting" your money, start to think of it as creating a money plan or a financial plan as an act of self-love.

Having a money plan means less stress and worry. You're not just winging it every single month and leaving your financial situation to chance. In a way, a money plan can make you a happier person because less stress = more happiness.

Day 19 Activity

Creating a good money plan could mean something as simple as spending your money smarter. This could mean prioritizing your wants and needs, and being strategic about how you spend your money in those areas. Answer the questions below:

1. List expenses that are your basic, unavoidable needs (rent, mortgage, utilities, etc.)

   _____
   _____
   _____

2. List some of the "wants" you currently spend money on but could potentially live without for the sake of bettering your money situation.

   _____
   _____
   _____

3. List the expenses (regardless of whether it is a need or want) that make you super happy.

   _____
   _____
   _____

Self-Love Tip: Spending money on experiences like vacations or meaningful things like charity or gifts for loved ones tend to make us happier.

Day 19 Thoughts and Understandings

Self-Love Note

"It's safe to use money to have all my needs met."

Make a Mini Vision Board for Your Dream Home

Home is definitely where the heart is, but it never hurts to visualize the type of house that you want to make into a home!

You might think that creating a vision board is silly. However, when you begin to understand that THOUGHTS BECOME THINGS, then you also understand the powerful significance of creating a visual aid such as a vision board.

Remember that everything that is and ever was started as a thought—a mere visualization before it became a reality.

Day 20 Activity

Visualize the dream home that you see yourself living in. To help, try searching Google or Pinterest for "dream home" images. You can also look through magazines and home buying guides to find something that catches your eye.

Cut out the picture and attach it here to this page. Then, close your eyes and imagine yourself living in that dream home. How does it feel? How will you decorate it? Will you have a house-warming party? Imagine it as clearly as if it were already a truth.

PASTE YOUR DREAM HOME IMAGE HERE

Day 20 Thoughts and Understandings

Self-Love Note

"It's safe for me to use money to create an easy life."

Day 21

Write Yourself a Check

There is power in writing out your goals. Monetary goals are no different.

What type of wealth would you like to attract into your life? What level of income do you see yourself making? Can you imagine what it would feel like to be completely financially secure?

Begin to visualize the exact amount of money you desire to be deposited in your bank account each month.

Mastering the Mindset of Self-Love

Day 21 Activity

Complete the following check by writing in the amount you want to manifest each month. Be sure to sign it and put the future date you intend to receive payment.

1. What steps are you willing to take towards accomplishing this money desire?

2. Do you have the potential to make this type of money in your current career?

3. If not, what career changes do you need to consider?

Day 21 Thoughts and Understandings

___

___

___

___

___

___

___

___

___

Self-Love Note

"Every day I am creating more wealth in my life."

Reflect on Your Spirituality

What is spirituality to you? When you were a child, spirituality was likely synonymous with religion. You were taught whatever it is your parents or caregivers were taught.

But as an adult, it's up to you to decide what spirituality means to you; to figure out who you are and what you believe. Spirituality is broad, and it has plenty of room for many perspectives.

Start by reflecting inward and connecting with your deepest beliefs and truths.

Day 22 Activity

List 3 major spiritual ideas or teachings you learned growing up.

1. _____
   _____

2. _____
   _____

3. _____
   _____

List 3 spiritual ideas you have come to understand outside of what you were previously taught that feel true to you.

1. _____
   _____

2. _____
   _____

3. _____
   _____

Spend some time today exploring what spirituality means to you. Write your definition of spirituality.

_____
_____
_____

Day 22 Thoughts and Understandings

Self-Love Note

"All spiritual practice is the art of shifting perspectives." - Teal

Create Calm in Your Day

Meditation is one of the many ways to bring yourself closer to your spirit. It doesn't necessarily mean meditating for extremely long periods of time. It can be achieved by simply taking 5 minutes to close your eyes and focus on one thing such as your breathing or even a song you enjoy.

The benefits of meditation are endless. Learning to calm your mind can allow you to see or hear the answer to a question you've been seeking or find the best solution to a problem you would like to solve.

Day 23 Activity

Below are nine types of meditation. Research each type and write a few notes on your understanding of that meditation. Next, decide on a few to try out for yourself. See which ones help you achieve the level of inner peace you need to begin transforming your life.

1. Zazen Meditation (yes/no)
_____
_____
_____

2. Mantra Meditation (yes/no)
_____
_____
_____

3. Metta Meditation (yes/no)
_____
_____
_____

4. Guided Visualization (yes/no)
_____
_____
_____

5. Mindfulness (yes/no)
_____
_____
_____

6. Heart Rhythm Meditation (yes/no)
_____
_____
_____

7. Transcendental Meditation (yes/no)
_____
_____
_____

8. Yoga Meditation (yes/no)
_____
_____
_____

9. Qi Gong Meditation (yes/no)
_____
_____
_____

Day 23 Thoughts and Understandings

_____

_____

_____

_____

_____

_____

_____

_____

_____

Self-Love Note

"The thing about meditation is: you become more and more you." - David Lynch

Understand Your Guiding Principles

Whether you find yourself facing good or bad circumstances, your guiding principles are what keep you grounded.

Having guiding principles can help you to make key decisions in your life. They provide the foundation to pursue goals in the most timely and effective way.

Your guiding principles are views that include your personal beliefs and values. They guide you throughout life and all its circumstances.

Do you understand your guiding principles? Are you moving towards those principles? If so, great. If not, it could mean you need to reinvent yourself.

Here are some ideas:

- Create and write out a vision statement
- Create and write out a mission statement
- Create and write out your guiding principles

Mastering the Mindset of Self-Love

Day 24 Activity

Create your vision, mission, and guiding principles.

1. Create and write your vision statement.

A vision statement can be a picture of your life in the future. It's your inspiration and framework for strategic life planning.

_____
_____

2. Create and write your mission statement.

A mission statement describes the purpose of your life. Your mission statement should guide your everyday actions. It should spell out your goals, provide a clear path and guide your decision making.

_____
_____

3. Establish guiding principles.

Guiding principles describe the beliefs and philosophy that guide what you do, why you do it, and how it gets done.

Guiding Principle #1 _____

Guiding Principle #2 _____

Guiding Principle #3 _____

Guiding Principle #4 _____

Day 24 Thoughts and Understandings

_____

_____

_____

_____

_____

_____

_____

_____

_____

_____

Self-Love Note

"Important principles may, and must, be inflexible." - Abraham Hicks

Ask the Universe for What You Want

When you go out to eat, you tell the waiter exactly what you want, and you expect to get that exact meal. The same holds true of asking the Universe. You should ask for exactly what you want.

You are limitless. Boundless. You are pure potential energy. There is a power inside of you that is beyond imagination. Knowing how to ask for what you want is one of the key ingredients of manifesting your dreams. You must make a specific request in a firm and clear way.

By asking, you are throwing a powerful boomerang out into the universe. Just like throwing an actual boomerang, when you throw it out there you also know that it is coming back to you very soon.

Day 25 Activity

7 steps to ask the Universe for what you want:

1. Relax your mind.

2. Be sure of what you want and have no doubt about receiving it.

3. Ask the Universe for it. Try saying, *"Universe, we are co-creating this life together. Continue to support me in manifesting (put your request here). Thank you for satisfying my request."*

4. Write your request down.

_____
_____
_____

5. Sit down, close your eyes and imagine yourself having what you asked for. Feel it as if you already have it.

6. Show gratitude. Thank the Universe for fulfilling you request. Even if you don't have it yet. Write your thank you message.

_____
_____
_____

7. Trust the Universe.

Day 25 Thoughts and Understandings

_____
_____
_____
_____
_____
_____
_____
_____
_____

Self-Love Note

"Ask for what you want and be prepared to get it." - Maya Angelou

Day 26

Living Intentionally

The Beatles said it best, "All you need is love, love. Love is all you need." If we were to set our daily intention to respond to life's happenings with nothing but love, it would nearly guarantee that we would begin to live a miraculous life.

Make it one of your life goals to live intentionally. Don't just react to situations. Instead, take the time to respond calmly by thinking things through and being intentional with your actions.

Instead of focusing on the worst possible outcomes, ask yourself, "What's the best that can happen?"

Here are some quick actions to begin living intentionally:

- Meditation to clear your thoughts
- Slow, deep breathing to relax
- Consistent actions
- Expressing gratitude for the now and the future

Mastering the Mindset of Self-Love

Day 26 Activity

Lay the foundation for an intentional life.

Design your perfect day. Write what that day would be like.
_____
_____
_____
_____
_____

Life is made up of choices. Every morning is a new day full of decisions. Pick your attitude. Write down what kind of attitude you will choose on a daily basis.
_____
_____
_____
_____

Do you normally choose to react or respond when life throws you a curve ball? Explain why.
_____
_____
_____
_____

Day 26 Thoughts and Understandings

Self-Love Note

"The difference between who you are and who you want to be is what you do."

Day 27

Discover Rituals That Serve You

What can you incorporate into your everyday life that will help you love yourself more? How about daily rituals?

Whether you know it or not, you perform rituals on a daily basis. From brushing your teeth to reading bedtime stories to taking a walk after dinner to meditating in the mornings. These are rituals if you do them consistently.

A ritual is an observance or practice that is performed the same way each time. Rituals are not just what you do but also how you do them. If your intention is to get closer to your spirit, then making a regular practice of living intentionally and with awareness will bring you closer to the person you want to be. The more time you spend interacting with your spirit, the stronger your relationship with your highest self will be.

Here are some ritual ideas:

- Ritual for cleaning
- Ritual for writing
- Ritual for eating
- Ritual for self-talk

Day 27 Activity

How to start a ritual:

List one ritual you can begin practicing today.

1._____

When beginning a ritual, it's important to start with the right intention. Focus your mind on your desire and commit to self-improvement. Think about what objective you wish to achieve. Create an intention that supports that objective. *(i.e. For a clean eating ritual, my intention is to be a blessing to my body. All my thoughts, words and actions reflect being a blessing to my body.)*

Write your intention.

_____
_____
_____

Write the thoughts associated with that intention.

_____
_____
_____

Write the actions associated with that intention.

_____
_____
_____

How many times a day will you perform your ritual(s)?

1   2   3

What times in the day will you perform your ritual(s)?

1st time _____   2nd time _____   3rd time _____

Day 27 Thoughts and Understandings

___

Self-Love Note

"The secret to your future is hidden in your daily routine." - Mike Murdock

Transform Your Life Through Beliefs

Some of us grew up with believing in superstition. Break a mirror--7 years bad luck. Step on a crack--break your mother's back.

What we think, say, and do determine the beliefs that create our reality. For this reason, you should choose beliefs that will benefit you in every area of your life--career, health, relationships or whatever it may be.

It's also a great idea to get rid of any beliefs that no longer serve your life purpose or those that scare you more than they help you.

Choose new beliefs that will serve every aspect of who you are and who you are becoming.

Here are some examples:

- I believe everyone I encounter will positively influence my life.
- I believe all things are working for the greater good of my life.
- I believe my inner Spirit is always guiding me to the right people and the right places.
- I believe every situation deserves to have a loving response.

Day 28 Activity

Write five beliefs that inspire you to transform into the person you want to become.

1. I believe_____.

2. I believe_____.

3. I believe_____.

4. I believe_____.

5. I believe_____.

Day 28 Thoughts and Understandings

_____
_____
_____
_____
_____
_____
_____
_____
_____
_____

Self-Love Note

"Believe life is worth living and your belief will help create the fact." - William James

Mastering the Mindset of Self-Love

50 Self-Love Affirmations

Today, I choose me.

I love my body and all it does for me.

My inner world creates my outer world.

I am worthy of love.

I carry strength and resilience with me.

My every step is one of courage.

I have the ability to overcome any challenge life gives me.

Abundance and love flow from me.

I am pure beauty.

I am a radiant and joyous person.

I am enough.

I am surrounded by the loving energy of the Universe.

I am loved beyond comprehension.

I am fierce.

My body, mind, and soul are the pictures of perfect health.

I am balanced.

I honor my inner voice.

I am abundant.

I am safe. I am supported. I am protected.

I am never alone. The universe supports me and is with me at every step.

I choose to be grateful for all that I have.

I am powerful beyond my wildest dreams.

My voice is valuable, and my opinion matters.

The universe is conspiring to help me succeed.

I am delightful.

I am not afraid to feel my feelings.

My mind is filled only with loving, healthy, positive and prosperous thoughts.

Mastering the Mindset of Self-Love

I consciously release the past and live only in the present.

I attract wonderful people into my life.

I am a magnet of love.

I am worthy of infinite and unending compassion.

My life is a celebration of my accomplishments.

I am successful.

Life is filled with joy and abundance.

Happiness flows freely from me.

Compassion is infinite and fully surrounds me and my life.

I am centered, peaceful, and grounded.

Love rises from my heart in the face of difficulty.

The love within me flows through me in every situation.

I am powerful, confident, and capable of reaching all my dreams.

I feel profound empathy and love for others and their unique paths.

I honor my life path.

I always have and will continue always to try my best; I honor this.

Success is defined by my willingness to keep going.

I walk this world with grace.

My body is a beautiful expression of my individuality.

I am authentic, true, and expressive.

I have the strength to rise in the face of adversity.

I have an infinite capacity for love and affection.

Love brings me youthfulness, energy, and rejuvenates me.

Mastering the Mindset of Self-Love

18 Money Mantras

Money comes easily, frequently, and abundantly.

I am a money magnet.

I am worthy of making more money.

Money simply falls into my lap.

My business is growing, expanding, and thriving.

Manifesting more money comes naturally.

The universe is conspiring to make me wealthy.

My positive attitude is attracting money.

Money comes to me in expected and unexpected ways.

I move from poverty thinking to abundance thinking.

I embrace new avenues of income.

My actions create constant prosperity.

I am thankful for the abundance and prosperity in my life.

Prosperity within me, prosperity around me; abundance within me, abundance around me.

I am a magnet for money. Prosperity is drawn to me.

There is no limit to the amount of money I am capable of earning.

I am open and receptive to all the wealth life offers me.

The universe always serves my highest interest.

Additional Self-Love Resources

Try these recommended resources to aid you in your self-love journey.

Mindset Book Recommendations

TheGorgeousMindsetEffect.com/Recommended-Reading

Spirituality and Soul Courses

Soulvana.com

Brea Cross Hall

BrighterFocus.com

Kristin Iris

IgniteThriveCreative.com

Kenya Jackson-Saulters

OutdoorJournalTour.com

Keep the Inspiration Going

Use the following pages to add more self-love ideas, tips, and inspiration.

_____
_____
_____
_____
_____
_____
_____
_____

Mastering the Mindset of Self-Love

Mastering the Mindset of Self-Love

About the Authors

Lani Edmonds is a motivational speaker, mindset coach, and co-founder of The Gorgeous Mindset Effect. She's a busy mom of 5 who knows first-hand the transformational power of having a positive mindset. She's an avid reader of Lisa Nichols, Tao Lopez, and Bob Proctor. Her motto for life: "What's The Best That Can Happen?"

Kari Sayers is a writer, creative energy coach, and co-founder of The Gorgeous Mindset Effect. Currently, she's on an adventure in Canada with her husband and two sons. She's a positivity enthusiast who believes in the power of positive thoughts. Her most recent published works include the Think Positive 30 Day Journal and Have You Seen My Sexy.

Visit www.TheGorgeousMindsetEffect.com for more inspiration.

Made in the USA
Middletown, DE
14 April 2018